INTERVIEW TIPS AND TECHNIQUES

A COMPREHENSIVE GUIDE ON HOW TO
SUCCEED IN AN INTERVIEW AND GET YOUR
DREAM JOB

Sarah Johnson

Contents

Introduction

This interview tips and techniques book will not only provide you with the knowledge you need to excel in your job interviews, it will help you nail your next interview so you get the job. It will discuss preparation for the interview, making a first impression, behavior during the interview, behavioral interview questions asked during an interview and how to answer them. What questions you should be asking, common mistakes and how to avoid them, and how to appropriately follow up post interview.

The book is aimed at both newbie and experienced people from all sectors, you will learn to understand the fundamentals of any interview so you can rise above the rest and stand out from the crowd. As you will soon understand when you read the book, you will be surprised, particularly the more experienced folks on how to plan and prepare for a solid and successful interview. You get one chance to show that you are the right candidate and if you follow the tips and techniques in this interview book, you will have given yourself every chance to be chosen for that dream job.

Times have certainly changed, and so have the requirements and expectations of employers; what was acceptable or applicable a few years ago may not be so in the modern age. This also means that hiring practices are no longer the same. Ultimately, when it comes to nailing a job interview, knowledge is power and preparation is key – that will never change. The question then becomes how can one adapt to changing hiring practices and ace a job interview in the current climate? What are the things one should know and how can one be best prepared? Read on to get answers.

5 Good reasons why this book should help you

1. It will help you to stand out in any job interview
2. It will help you land your dream job
3. It will show you how to answer Interview questions
4. It will show you what to do and what not to do in an interview
5. This book will truly show you how to rise above the rest to get that dream job!

Short book brief

The following chapters provide a synthesis of everything you need to know about making the most out of this crucial part of the job application process. Lots of the information may seem obvious to some but that's the point, as human beings we need to understand the regimental approach to job interviews and how to go about them.

When I say regimental it is literally that, do this, do that, remember this, say this. Being structured and regimental in your approach will cover all angles so that you are successful. I mention on numerous occasions that for the most part, folks turn up to interviews just expecting their CV or Resume to do the work for them, this is a big mistake. Interviewers want to be sold to, they want you to show your character and skills, they want you to sell yourself and make the interview easy for them.

It really does not matter if you are interviewing for a part time role or a high end management role, you need to be prepared and sell yourself. This book will ingrain all relevant requirements so that you fly through your interviews and leave nothing off the table.

There are literally hundreds of thousands of people who are on the hunt for a new job every single day. To many, finding a new job can be one of the most stressful occasions in your working life. It can be tiring and mentally challenging. Your confidence can take a bashing if you do not experience early success.

You will be taught step by step on how to nail that interview to land your dream job. These are actionable tips and ways which will prepare you both physically and mentally for the interview process. You will learn how to create great first impressions, stay composed and stand on your feet to give great responses. You will also be taught on how to best present yourself in a way which will make you stand out from the crowd and be noticed.

Chapter 1: Understanding Job Interviews

Ok, so you are either applying for a job so you want to prepare in advance which is a great move, as you should be prepared in advance. Or, after sending out numerous job applications and patiently waiting, you've finally got the much anticipated call to go for an interview with a potential employer.

Having managed to get a job interview means you have surpassed countless other applicants vying for the job, and are among the shortlisted candidates deemed qualified to fill the position. You are being given the chance to convince a potential employer firsthand that you are the person their organization needs. As such, you want to be sure to make the most out of this golden opportunity by putting your best foot forward and, hopefully, secure the job you want.

Job Interviews: Then vs. Now

In the not-so-distant past, people were oftentimes introduced to job openings through being referred by someone or by browsing the classified advertisements in newspapers. Competition was not as though, and if you were lucky enough to be referred by someone the employer knew and trusted, you were likely to already have an advantage over the other candidates.

However, when the internet became the main outlet for recruitment and job searching in the new millennium, it changed the game. Job applicants began to have easier access to information on who was hiring, leading to a significantly higher response to job postings. Recruiters were then faced with the overwhelming task of sorting through hundreds, maybe even thousands, of applications and narrowing down potential candidates to a small handful. The selected few would then have to go through a tough interview process until the suitable candidate was found from among the hopefuls.

It is hardly a surprise that recruiters have changed their interviewing practices, and now take a tougher approach when screening for suitable candidates. Thus, job seekers now have additional criteria to fulfill in addition to simply stating their credentials, if they want to land that dream job in today's increasingly competitive environment.

What a Recruiter Wants

A job interview is a twofold process. On one hand, a potential employer will be gauging whether you have the capacity to competently fulfill the required role. The interview also allows for a company to form a well-rounded impression of whether a candidate has the personality and motivation to succeed in the particular industry for which they are interviewing. On the other hand, an interviewee has the opportunity to assess whether joining the organization is in line with their career goals, and is also given the chance to convince the hiring manager as to why they are the right fit for a job opening.

Perhaps the most baffling aspect of job hunting is figuring out exactly what recruiters are looking for. More importantly though, how can one get ahead of the pack to become that one outstanding candidate from many who actually lands the job?

The profile of an ideal employee differs from employer to employer. However, the basic tenets of having integrity, the drive to excel and the ability to learn quickly will generally get one noticed, especially if one has ambitions of climbing the corporate ladder. Even though there is no doubt that hard work, perseverance and diligence are essential qualities for success in any job, there are qualities outside of credentials and experience that will get the attention of employers – namely, attitude and mindset.

Businesses are facing various intense challenges in the current economy and market place. This increased competition has meant that companies now need to be lean and efficient. Thus, oftentimes they need employees who can do more than simply perform one particular function in the company. Favorable candidates are the ones who demonstrate creativity, commitment and passion to the job, showing that they are adaptable in a fast-paced working environment and are able to contribute to the business growth agenda in the industry for the long-run.

In summation, as a job seeker, your career survival and progression depends on how much you can contribute to an organization besides what is already specifically requested in the job description. The job interview is a window of opportunity in which you should be aiming to convince a potential employer that, not only can you fulfill the job requirements, but you can bring more to the table than what is being requested.

Chapter 2: Preparing For Job Interviews

To prepare for a job interview you will need:

- A computer, tablet or mobile device with access to the internet
- A notepad and pen, or note taking software (e.g. MS Word) to make notes
- The Job description. If you don't have one of these then ask! It's very difficult to prepare without one
- The names and positions of people who will be interviewing you

Research the company where you are applying for the role

Start by going to the company's main website. If you don't have the website address use a search engine like Google to find the address by entering the name of the company and its location. Normally, on company websites you can find an 'About us' section that contains a brief history of the company along with a description of their products and services. Some companies also post videos on their web sites or link to a YouTube channel. Videos may include interviews with employees of the company or information about products and services.

Prepare examples from your personal experience

The best answer to any question during a job interview is an answer that is backed up with examples from your personal experience. This is especially true when you are asked questions about difficult or awkward situations, such as "What would you do if a client refuses to pay for the work?" or "What would you do if your subordinate didn't turn up for work and won't answer the phone?"

Prepare A Good CV Or Resume

A CV (curriculum vitae) or resume is your first pass selling tool!. A CV is a more detailed version of your skills and experience where as a resume is more of a one or two page summary. However, what you will find is that both terms are used in the same way or for the same purpose. CV is short for curriculum vitae and mainly a term used in the United Kingdom, whereas Resume is more a term used in the US, to keep it simple, they both in essence have the same meaning. For the purpose of this book we are going to use the term CV. Now a good CV is what represents you when you are seeking a job. It talks about you in a manner you wouldn't be able to explain in a personal interview.

It is the prima facie evidence of your credentials and displays your potential to those who are in a position to award you a job. It is of paramount importance that you start working towards building a good CV right from your student days. Interning at good places, presenting papers on your subjects and working under experienced and renowned people from your field, are some of the very significant things that a competitive CV should contain. If you did not go the education route, list all your working skills, any volunteering experience, or any sporting club past times where you got involved, lead, helped, etc.

Think of some questions you can ask your interviewer

Show interviewers that you are interested by asking about what you read on the company's website. For example, you could ask them about the company's plans for the future or whom they see as their main competitors. During your interview you will be asked if you have any questions, please, please do not sit there and say no!.

Research the company, the people, their history! After all, it is your future as well.

The day before the interview, refresh your memory

It's best to do items 1-5 above around 2-3 days before the interview. This gives all the new information time to settle in your mind. The day before the job interview, read all the notes that you took while preparing. Read the job description one more time and make sure that you understand every single word. Read the information that you noted about your interviewers.

Relax and get some rest before the interview

After you finish the preparation, put all the materials and notes away and try not to think about the interview for at least 3-4 hours before going to sleep.

You've done all of the preparation already and now it is important to get enough rest and sleep in order to feel your best during the interview.

The best way to take your mind off the interview is to read a book or watch an interesting film. It is best not to drink any alcohol the evening before your interview as you will be less alert during the following day.

Create a Personal Folder

A personal folder is a collection of documents that pick up where your resume ends. It provides a more complete picture of you as a person than can fit on a resume. As an added benefit, it is nice to have the ability to look back at all of your past projects and accomplishments.

This folder can be a physical collection of documents or it can be saved in a digital format. If it is in digital form, make sure you take a device to the interview that can adequately display the content for the potential employer. You do not want to attempt to show them your achievements and projects on a phone screen.

Chapter 3: Interview Dress Code

Carefully consider the work environment. There are very few places you will get a job if you show up wearing something you'd wear to do work in the backyard.

If you want to be hired as a supervisor, dress as an executive. And so on. When in doubt at all, a business suit, for men and women, works for just about every interview. And be conservative. A gray, black, or navy suit is more appropriate than red or purple or some other bright color.

The minute you step inside the interview room, your interviewer starts sizing you up based on the way you are dressed. Like it or not, you will be creating an immediate impression on his/her mind as to the kind of person you are by looking at what you are wearing.

If you show up fresh, polished, and properly dressed, the image that will pop up naturally in your interviewer's mind is that of a person who took extra effort to look good for the interview. Dressing up well for the interview will not only make you stand out from the rest of the pack, it also gives you an extra-ordinary 'feel good' feeling which heightens your enthusiasm and self-confidence.

To put this into perspective for you, I guarantee that if you dress up extremely nice for a fancy date you feel much more positive and confident within yourself as opposed to when you just go on a date to the movies with someone and you just dress in casual clothes.

As far as rules concerning dressing up for a job interview is concerned, nothing is really carved in stone. No two company is the same in what they consider as the acceptable dress code for an interview. So, your best option is to simply dress for success. It is not really that difficult in deciding what interview outfit to choose for that big day.

Here are some useful tips you can use on how to dress up for a job interview:

- Do some online sleuthing to find out what the dress code is in the company. Visit the company's website and see if there are photos or videos posted there. By watching the videos, you'd be able to get an idea on the over-all atmosphere prevailing in the company. Fashion yourself appropriately.

- Try to dress up just a tad higher than what people in the company wear. Don't worry about appearing overdressed for the occasion if you look fresh, polished, and properly dressed. The important thing is to create a lasting impression on the interviewer.

- Make sure you look neat. Never show up in ill-fitting, or wrinkled clothes. Bring a grooming kit with you and step into the comfort room to comb your hair and even brush your teeth if necessary. Do a last-minute look-over in front of the mirror before proceeding to the interview room.

- Keep your looks simple and not loud. You wouldn't want your interviewer to be distracted by anything other than your positive personality. Avoid using excessive jewelry, putting on thick makeup, neon-colored hair and fancy, skimpy clothing that shows too much skin. Bring a long a briefcase (or a handbag for the ladies). It will make you look neat and organized.

- Avoid using perfume especially those that have powerful scents. It won't help your cause instead, it will only distract the interviewer who may even be sickened by its puissant scent. In the first place, you would want to be remembered for your skill sets and experience and not for the stench of your perfume.

- Do a dress rehearsal a day before the interview to make sure everything fts perfectly. This will give you time to make some changes or adjustments where ever they may be needed.

Chapter 4: The Interview Mindset

Why is the interview mindset so important? Simply because we live out who we believe we are. We act out our self-given identity. And if you don't see yourself as the most competent person that should be hired, there is no way you will act the part.

So what is the interview mindset? It is simply the mindset that seeks nothing from people and only for people.

It is only when you don't seek anything from people, be it their attention, their adoration, their acceptance. It's only when you don't need that will you even have a chance of earning it. People are repelled by neediness, perhaps because they see themselves in it. But when they come across somebody who is confident, secure, and not needing of people's adoration, people begin to notice.

And then to seal the deal, when this confident person is not only self-sufficient, but seeks the good of others, people cannot help but be drawn in. Why? Because this is counterintuitive. It's not normal. But when you learn how to master this mindset, you learn how to win people.

The reality is, people like, trust, hire, and follow people that:

- They like and admire
- Like and are interested in them
- Are similar to them

We're going to break this mindset into five principles or the five pillars that create this mindset.

It is crucial that you develop these mental habits overtime to master life's interviews.

Be the Leader

Be the leader. Even when you're not. Display authority, even when you don't have it. The truth is, you don't need an actual position of leadership to give off a sense of influence. Not at all. Leadership happens when you come across as somebody who knows what he or she's doing. Somebody with an established sense of self and purpose.

In the interview room, this looks like you displaying confidence in yourself. It means walking into the interview with the mindset that your time is limited and valuable, you have other options (or will have them), you know that this company desperately needs to fill this position, and you'll give them some time to sell it to you.

Be Knowledgeable

You can tell immediately who the leader in the room is by seeing who everybody naturally turns to when a question is asked. Even if they don't have the official position of authority. Why? Because they're the most likely to know the answer. And those who know are those we follow.

Be an Expert Affirmer

The natural disposition of a person is to live a self-absorbed life. It's a sad reality, but as I mentioned in the first few pages of this book, that's how I lived.

As human beings, we are all naturally self-centered and overly self-conscious. Call it psychology, or evolutionary traits, or sin, or whatever worldview you come from, we cannot deny this fact. But we can use it to our advantage.

Get in Their World

This principle deals with the last type of person that people like: People that are like them. If you've ever been a new place, whether traveling, or a new school, or a new job, who do you gravitate towards?

It could be anything from how they dress, their ethnicity, their personality, etc. And when you start to get to know people more, you're drawn even closer to those who share similar interests as you, whether hobbies, or religion, or past experiences.

Those with the interview mindset know this well and will do everything to make these connections. When these connections are made, hiring managers are 50% more likely to remember your name.

Be Reserved

This is a common human characteristic and it's often exhibited in the movies we watch. All of the leaders that are portrayed as respected are also portrayed as slightly mysterious and reserved, as if they always know something we don't and we can trust them for that. Take note that it's not that we are borrowing from the movies and fantasy. Instead, it's the reserve. The movies simply portray the characteristics of human nature. We look up to leaders that seem to always know what they're doing and are reserved and humble about it.

Nerves and Anxiety

Depending on your general day to day confidence level, nerves and anxiety can creep into your mindset. It is absolutely natural to have some form of anxiety prior to any major occasion including interviews. There is no exact answer to conquer these feelings as each human being is unique. To keep it simple, if you have prepared correctly, done your homework! Then reality is, you are going for a well-informed chat with a bunch of people who are going to give you that job you really want. Enjoy your interview! Yes, enjoy it, it's about you, be proud, be happy, be positive.

One funny example my Mother in law used to tell me was, when she went for interviews and entered the room, if she felt any anxiety she used to visualize the folks around the interview table naked! I know, I know, but it gets worse, she use to visualize the interviewers naked wearing clown bow ties that spun round! It used to make me laugh but guess what, I used to do exactly that and still to this day thank my Mother in law for such an idea. It's a crazy example but why not, if that what makes anyone feel at ease then so be it. The point of mentioning this is, just remember, you are a great person, the folks around that interview table are no better or worse than you. We are all human beings, take away the suits, the ties, the overalls or whatever, we are all the same, so please don't forget that. You are a great person and you have done your homework, you are ready to nail this interview!.

Chapter 5: How to Handle Yourself During an Interview

As you might expect, the actual interview is a critical part of this entire process. Let's take a look at some topics to consider at this pivotal moment.

Be confident in yourself. If you have landed an interview, the company has already seen promise in you. Now you just have to build upon that and show them what personal advantages you can bring to their business.

First impressions leave a lasting impression so be sure to represent yourself well. Looking them in the eyes and giving a firm handshake is an undervalued way to set yourself apart from the competition.

Smile. A company wants to know that you are going to be a nice, as well as a capable, coworker. Simply smiling can ease any tension in the interview and guide it to a more positive atmosphere.

If they mention that you are under qualified in some way, acknowledge any true statements and then pivot the conversation to a more positive stance. This is usually how you plan to correct the issue or move onto something that you consider to be equivalent experience.

As expected, an interviewer will ask the applicant questions during the interview process. However, the prepared and successful job seeker should also pose questions back to the prospective company.

This is a fantastic way to show the potential employer that you are an above average candidate. A lot of candidates do not ask employers very many questions and you will stand out from the crowd if you do. Asking detailed questions shows the employer that you are a candidate who is taking the opportunity seriously.

A master question list is a helpful way of ensuring that all of the important details are discussed when under the pressure of an interview. Maintaining these in a spreadsheet or a bulleted list of these questions is recommended to keep them all neatly organized in one location. You will have to choose which questions are applicable to each interview because each one is a unique experience.

Two things to never do are chew gum or mints and use slang in speech. It is unattractive, you cannot hide it and it is rude. Never have things in your mouth during an interview. Speak well and intelligently. You do not want to come off as unintelligent or unprofessional or even just rude.

There are things you should pay close attention to that can make a huge different in your impression on the interviewer.

Confidence

You must come into an interview with confidence. No one wants to hear whining or see someone that clearly does not believe they cannot do the job. This is a delicate balance because you do not want to be too cocky. You want to be sure of yourself, but not flamboyant about it. The interviewer should know that you are capable of doing the job but will also get along well with your co-workers.

Accomplishments should be factual. You want to list them as a matter-of-fact without a great amount of detail. The interviewer needs to know what they are, but you do not need to brag.

Attitude

Positive attitudes are more alluring than negative ones. You want to smile and be a happy individual to talk to. Remember that you are trying to sell yourself to the interviewer. Avoid frowning and looks of disdain if you hear something that is not what you expected or wanted. Wait for the appropriate time to discuss concerns.

Eye Contact

You want to maintain eye contact with the person you are talking to otherwise you appear insecure or rude. You do not want to come off as uninterested as this is the person deciding if you will get the job. You would not appreciate this type of behavior from someone else so do not do look around the room.

Chapter 6: Latest Behavioral Interview Questions and Answers

Regardless of who you are or what position you're interviewing for, there are some fairly common questions that come up in most interviews. The answers are important not for what they really say but for demonstrating how you think and react. The following are some of the most common questions and some tips on how to answer them without putting yourself in a bad light.

Why do you want this job?

Companies really want to hire people who are passionate about the job, so you should have a great answer about why you really want the position. First, identify a couple of key elements that make the role a great fit for you, for example, "I love human resources because I love the constant human interaction and the fulfillment that comes from helping people solve a problem". This could be just about anything, it could be for a journalist role, or photographer, etc., etc. Then share why you love your job or industry and your potential new company (e.g., "I've always been passionate about education (whatever field you are in), and I think you're doing great things, so I really want to be a part of it").

Describe your greatest success?

This question is most common for people seeking managerial or higher jobs, but it can come up for anyone. What this question is really asking is, "Are you just a warm body collecting a paycheck or can I expect you to do something of value?"

Simply put, if you were something other than a warm body, you've done something at your job. So tell them about it. And if you really haven't, an answer like, "While I haven't yet been a part of any company or department decisions or accomplishments, I've proven myself to be a reliable worker and look forward to when I will be helping to make those decisions."

Describe your greatest failure?

If your greatest failure was forgetting to take aluminum foil out of the microwave and starting a fire that burned down the company building, it's best not to mention it. This question is really asking what sort of adversity have you faced and how did you overcome it.

Good answers for this include not speaking up or voicing your opinion about how something could have been improved or done better, or not reacting quickly enough to what you could see was a personality conflict or even departmental conflict that escalated or festered. If you were a person in charge, it could be something like making a decision for your department with input from everyone but your department members.

Remember, the key to this question is not the answer, it's how you learned from the failure. The worst mistake is one that's repeated.

What was your greatest obstacle?

This is very similar to the last question, and the key again is not the obstacle but how you overcame it and how that's made you a better employee.

Good answers for this question include common complaints in your line of work. Maybe your line of work often misses deadlines, so your greatest obstacle might be frequently missing deadlines but how you manage to get things done early or have learned to anticipate last-minute problems so that this is no longer a concern for you.

Where do you see yourself in five years?

This question seems simple, but the answer you give reveals two things. First, the interviewer is trying to find out if you have any ambition or if you're happy being where you are. In other words, if you're hired in at the bottom rung on the ladder, will you be content to stay there? The other thing is subtle. Specifically, the interviewer wants to know if you're using this job as a springboard to something else or if this is a long-term company hire. Your answer should alleviate both concerns.

For example, if you're being hired as a factory worker, store clerk, or office worker, your answer might be something like, "In five years I'd like to see myself with new and improved skills in this field. I'd also like to know that as I've improved myself on the job it has been noticed and I've acquired more responsibility." This shows that you're not looking to gain a skill to move to somewhere else while also indicating that you want to learn more and be a better worker. In short, you're a long-term employee they will want.

Why are you looking to leave your current position?

If you are currently employed, you will likely be asked this question. Your answer will determine if they want to take a chance on you, someone who might be a job hopper. You answer needs to assure them that you are a good hire.

- If your company is struggling financially and has had layoffs, state that. And tell them that you saw the current opportunity as a good one for you (and your family, if applicable) and didn't want to wait around until your position was caught in a round of reductions in force.

- If you're leaving because of a personality conflict with your boss, couch it in terms that don't make you seem like a terrible person to supervise. Answer that your current department was going in a direction that didn't allow you to be the best employee you could be, so you wanted to take the opportunity with another company where you could use your skills and abilities to their fullest.

- If you're leaving for a promotion, you are free to say so. But not with bald ambition. Answer something to the effect of, "There are limited growth opportunities at my current position.

What do you think of our company? Did you look at our website?

This is a basic "due diligence" question. In other words, do you know what you're getting into. If you're going to a larger company, your answer can focus on the company's position as a market leader, its brand recognition, or the opportunity to work for a reputable company in your area.

Your answer can be mostly the same if you're going to an older company. If you're going to a smaller company, you can focus more on how the smaller atmosphere makes you feel more valuable and not just an employee number. If you're going to a newer company, opportunities for growth, the chance to be part of something new and exciting, or similar wording should be part of your answer. Also be sure to include in your answer some knowledge of the company's flagship products or services.

What is your greatest strength?

This is a tired question, but it still is out there. If there is ever a time to toot your own horn, this question gives it to you. However, you must toot reasonably. The interviewer wants to know what you're bringing to the table, and they want to know that you bring it and can still fit your head through the doorway.

Whichever strength you have, be sure that you relate that strength to being effective at your job. It's not a strength to know the score of every football game played in the last two seasons if the position you're interviewing for is a copy machine repairman.

When can you start?

If you are not currently working, answering that you can start when you are hired is perfectly acceptable. But if you are currently working, your answer should be along the lines of, "I could start right away, but I'd prefer to give my current employer two weeks' notice." This satisfies any concerns the hiring manager might have about your calling in "I quit" on a Monday morning while also allowing for an immediate need to be met.

What are your strengths?

Name the qualities that you possess and believe are the most useful for the role you are applying for. It's better to back up your words with examples from your personal experience – tell them about your achievements at your previous job. For example, tell them about processes you improved and/or how you increased the profits of the company.

What are your weaknesses?

This is a tricky question. Don't try to show that you are open and honest and begin naming all your negative qualities. Instead transform negative into positive. For example, you can say that you never give up until you finish something and, therefore, often stay at work until late. You can also say that you feel that you could top up your knowledge on a subject that complements your profession but is not a core part of it. Ensure you mention that you are already making efforts to improve in this area through your own pro-activity.

Why do you think that you are good for this role?

Show your knowledge of the company, your interest in its products and services and how your skills will help to support them. Demonstrate that you are knowledgeable about the industry and market in which the company operates, and express a desire to build a career in that industry.

Did you ever make mistakes in your previous job?

Tell them only about the small mistakes you made, what you did to fix the situation, and what lessons you learned from the experience. Don't blame other people. Show that you are capable of admitting your mistakes and can quickly and effectively put things right again.

How do you like to spend your free time?

It's not only important to show that you have a few different hobbies (e.g. photography, swimming, horse riding etc.), but also to show that your profession is one of your main interests and that you spend a lot of time on self-development and improving your skills (reading books, attending courses and seminars etc.

What relationship do you have with your colleagues?

If you have very few or no people reporting to you then you should show that you are a team player and that you are capable of taking the initiative. Also mention that you enjoy helping your colleagues to achieve better results.

If you are applying for a higher management position then you need to show that you can manage people effectively and know how to get the best results from them, while maintaining a good relationship with employees.

Why have you had so many short projects?

This is a question mainly for freelancers, say from the oil and gas industry. As a freelancer, you obviously go from project to project. Ideally you would love to hold a project for 2-3 years at a time but that's not always possible.

Sometimes folks who are interviewing you will note that your CV shows a number of short term roles, they will want to ask you why? It could imply that perhaps you do not fit into companies very well, and or you tend to jump ship for higher rates every chance you can. Even if this is the case, as a self-employed freelancer you have to go where the money is, saying that projects don't always wait for you to come along!.

What usually happens is that unless you get lucky, you get hired either at the start to help set up the project, but when it is all looking good, good bye! It's time to hand over to the staff person and save money now that you have sorted out the problems. The other end of the scale is being hired towards the end of a project when folks are leaving for new projects or the project is in trouble.

The best answer is just tell it how it is, say that ideally you would have loved to have a string of 2-3 year projects but unfortunately you have not been lucky enough to get on projects from the start, or if you have, you were released so the staff person could take over, that's how it usually rolls. It works both ways, many companies have sat in front of a freelancer and told them there is a 2-3 year project for them.

Reality is, they know fine well that when you get through the hard work and all is ok, they will hand it over to the staff person so that they can either save money, or, in most cases they can charge out to end client the same rate but pay the staff person much less than you. Such as life, just remember to say how it is. You are a freelance business.

How do need to be managed?

Remember that you should always use positive words when answering this question, you want to show respect, but at the same time, you don't want to show that you can't do the job without someone guiding you all day.

For example:

"A leader who I can learn from and will give me an opportunity to show my strengths. Someone who will be guiding me and supporting me with advice in difficult situations if required." Or, you could say something like:

" A manager who when I have proved myself will trust me to add value to the business by completing my tasks with minimal supervision."

These are the best answers to use, it shows that you are respectful, but also, you don't need to be hand held every day and that you are keen to do well.

What salary are you looking for?

There is no correct answer to this question. If you ask for too much then you may be considered an overly ambitious person, too little and you may sound under qualified. Bear in mind that, for the majority of companies, you will get the salary that you request for a whole year from the start date.

If you agree to salary that is below what you really want, then you may come to regret this during the next twelve months. It is better to choose the golden middle and add a little on top, leaving room for negotiation. The main tip here is, do your homework, why are you there in the first place? Have you been given a salary band? Have you done your research?

Salary, or rates for project workers or freelancers can differ. If you are a freelancer you should know pretty much what you want, or what the company will pay. It also has other variables such as, how long have you been out of work? Is your market niche booming or in decline?. I also talk about salary in chapter two.

What would you do if you encountered conflict in the workplace?

It is better to say that you always keep calm, neutral and try to focus on finding a solution to the conflict through discussion and diplomacy. Mention examples from your previous experience where you resolved conflict at work. The idea here is to show you won't PANIC and lose your cool!.

What did you like most in your previous role?

Here it is important to show your interest in the current role that you are applying for. Therefore, it is best to mention the aspects of your current job that will be present in the new role. Show that you like your profession and that you like working with people. You also need to highlight how you think the new company can make the job more enjoyable for you.

Do you have any questions for us?

Always prepare 2-3 questions for your interviewer – the most neutral questions are: How many people work in the department?

What are you plans for developing the company? How soon are you planning to make a decision about who to appoint in this position? We will cover general questions to ask in the next chapter.

Chapter 7: Questions You Should Ask if Given the Chance

After all is said and done, you are sometimes given the opportunity to ask questions of the interviewer. This opportunity should not be tossed away no matter how long the interview has gone on. Again, you are trying to find out as much about them as they are about you. Getting a job doesn't mean you'll enjoy it, and some jobs are better off being turned down if you can afford it. To help you along, here are a few questions you should ask when given the opportunity.

Is this a new position or a vacated one?

If the position was vacated when someone left, you need to know why. It could be simply that the person changed jobs within the company, moved out of the area, or received another job offer. If it's something more sinister, such as a serious personality conflict or they had to be "let go" for some undefined reason, this will warn you. You're not likely to find out details, but knowing that your position was opened because someone else was more or less forced to leave is an indicator that if you have another job offer, it might be preferable. Granted, the personality conflict or the reason a person was let go might be totally irrelevant to you because of your personality or skills or work ethic, but it might not. Forewarned is forearmed.

What do you like best about working here?

If you can ask this question of several people you will be doing well, but even getting an answer from one person will tell you a bit about the company culture. It might be something simple like free food or drinks, but it could also be something critical to enjoying your job like feeling as if you're a valued employee. Based on the answer or answers you get, you will have a very good idea if the things that make that company a good place to work are things you value and will make your employment there enjoyable.

What do you expect of the person you hire for this position?

Keep in mind as well that some managers will tell you in answer to this question how they plan on treating the new employee. Every manager checks on new employees pretty much daily, but what will it be like after you've been there a few weeks? Will the manager continue to check on you daily? Are there weekly meetings? Are you expected to ask questions when you need help and otherwise just keep the wheels of progress turning? What you hear hopefully aligns with what you want.

What would you expect me to accomplish in my first 3 months of working with you?

This is one question which the interviewer wants to ask but often fails to ask due to time constraints. If he fails to ask you this, then you should ask it yourself. By asking the interviewer this question, he will have the impression that you want to make a difference – that you want to hit the ground running.

Can you tell me what you consider as the top 3 personality traits your top performers have in common?

The answer to this question will give you an idea what the company views as the top qualities of their top performers. Asking this question suggests that you want to be a great employee too like their top performers. It could be that their top performers are highly creative, or they work longer hours, or they are consistent top sales performers.

Whatever the interviewer ventures for an answer will be good information for you to help you fit into the team as well as be one of the top performers too once they hire you.

What motivates people in your company to strive for excellence in their jobs?

Asking this question creates the impression that you are a candidate who is keen on helping the company succeed. What you want to find out is if there are any employee engagement program that makes a difference and drives results. The reason you ask this question is because you want to support the employee engagement program by living the company's values.

What are your highest-priority projects, and how would you like me to contribute to its success?

With this question, your interviewer will think of you as a very serious candidate who is not looking for just any job he can lay his hands on. Rather, the image you project with this question is that of a man with a purpose who seeks a job with meaning.

Chapter 8: Mind your body language

Remember that many employers not only know about body language, but also place as much importance on this as they do the content of your answers. The main indicators of someone being nervous or trying to disguise something are: suddenly changing your seating position (for example, when the interviewer asks an uncomfortable question), constantly touching your face, fiddling with your pen or other objects and shaking your leg.

So that you don't get distracted thinking about how you sit or what gestures you are making when talking, you should practice at home. Sit at a table and ensure that your back and neck are straight, shoulders are relaxed, lower arms are resting on the table and that you are sitting comfortably. Do not interlock your fingers as this can be seen as a sign that you are trying to hide something. Sit like this for a while and memorize this pose. Imagine that you are talking to the interviewer. This will help you to feel more confident and relaxed at the interview.

Facial Expressions

Your face says a lot about you. Without treading into the unsafe field of first impressions, your face is your entire profile in an interview. It is the first thing people notice when you walk into the room. Your mind, your intellect, your wit, your sense of humor; all come secondary to the onlookers' minds. It is your face that leads everything else.

Droopy eyes clearly indicate that the person is not interested in what is in front of him. It may, at times, even be offensive to some people. On the other hand, attentive and alert eyes signify that you are genuinely taking interest what the other person has to say. However, popping out eyes is a sign towards overacting. If a person's eyes follow the speaker's hand movement, blink at the right time intervals and do not have eye-sand in them, it leaves behind a good impression on the speaker.

Watch your mouth. Literally! The way you position your lips in an interview is vital towards indicating what mood you are in! If you have an open mouth, it shows that either you are dumbfounded by the conversation's contents or you are simply sitting there not listening to whatever's being said. On the other hand, if you use your lips to occasionally smile a little, it may encourage the interviewer to do more of what they are doing.

If you are twitching your lips, it indicates that you are under a bit of stress. Lip twitching has always been associated with nervousness. If you twitch your lips in a job interview, your chances of getting selected drop significantly, as it shows a lack of confidence.

Your eyebrows serve more purpose than simply completing your face. Use them to full advantage to show inquisitiveness. You can focus your eyebrows together to signify that you have not understood what has just been said. However, too much of squinting may backfire, as it will be overdoing it. You can show 'surprise' by raising your eyebrows, despite a certain English idiom appointing an entirely different interpretation to 'raising eyebrows.' Express shock or mild surprise by exploiting your eyebrows smartly.

Your facial expressions cover more than just your eyes, lips and eyebrows. It is how your face as a whole is presented that matters and not just its individual parts. When you have a smiling face, it is natural that those sitting right across the interview table feel good vibes coming from you. On the other hand, a face with a grimace on it is considered cold and unfriendly.

Body Postures

Body postures are all about how you carry yourself. It is the ultimate platform for your body language to be displayed in full vigor.

Sitting is as important as walking. Do not pull the chair out and just assume that you are to sit unless someone asks you to. It is not only against your prospects of landing a job, but also rude to sit down on your own as it gives off an aura of superiority. Wait for one of the interviewers to ask you to sit. Assume a straight posture, with your backbone touching the back of the chair at all points. Do not sit too stiff, as that could lead to cramps and make you nervous eventually.

Do not sit slouching. Straighten up your shoulders a bit and appear smart while doing so. Do not cross your legs under the table. Though most interviewers cannot see what is going on under the table, that position does affect your upper body. One can easily tell how casually your legs are placed under the table by taking a single glance at your upper body.

Do not place one leg above the other while sitting. It shows that you are not just confident about yourself, but also show a general attitude of carelessness towards the interviewers. Behave in a manner that sends the message that you respect them.

Sitting upright in an interview might go in favor of you since it displays an attentive mentality. On the other hand, adopting a slouching position signifies that you are in the mood to hear them out and are only there only to doodle and pass time.

Gestures

In an interview, if you are sitting in a cross-armed position, it implies that you are not welcome to others' point of views and ideas. It displays a cold attitude and often does not come off as desirable. On the other hand, instead of crossing arms, if you sit with your hands in your lap or on the table, you give off a friendly and warmer aura and it will definitely fetch you brownie points.

It is a sign of careless confidence to casually fling your arms around while walking. On the other hand, if you clench your fists and walk, it may imply that you are calculated and reserved about yourself.

Hands can be used to convey emotions too. Joining your hands in a Namaste sign shows that you mean respect towards the person. Bowing down is another form of respect followed by the Japanese. If you show someone the 'thumbs up' sign, it means that you are either wishing them good luck or are conveying 'okay' or one of its variants. However, if you do the same in other countries like Iran or Thailand; it can be taken as an equivalent of showing the middle finger in the West.

So, make sure you do not consciously or subconsciously offend your interviewers with your body language or gestures.

Handshakes

A very common way to greet each other is by shaking each other's hand. This has been a tradition since the medieval period. A handshake is supposed to signify greeting, completion, agreement or friendship and calling off of war.

In an interview, the first and only physical interaction you will have with your prospective employer is through the handshake that you perform when you first walk in. The way a person shakes his hand with others says a lot about him. If the handshake is firm, it means the person performing it is confident and is clear about his intentions.

On the other hand, if it's a loose handshake, it displays a lack of self-confidence and casualness. A weak handshake is often taken to be a sign towards half-agreement and not a full nod. Studies over the years have classified handshakes into various categories like the Bone Crusher – squeezing hands too hard, and the Limp Fish-weakly done handshake.

Biting your nails is a clear sign of anxiety. Though it is perfectly human to be anxious, remember it is a rat race competition out there. Interviewers will be hunting for people that are not going through their own personal issues already. Hence, it is advisable not to bite your nails and give them a chance to strike your name off the list.

Do not nod or shake your head at the wrong times. In a fit of frenzy and a rush to impress, many candidates fail to even grasp the question and simply nod or shake their head. A nod signifies yes and a mere shaking of head denotes no. If you have fully understood the question and are clear and ready to elucidate, only then must you nod or shake your head. Nodding and shaking of the head also comes under body language and must be sparingly used.

Make sure your feet are positioned properly. Feet that are placed in the direction of the door paint a very sorry picture of a candidate. It indicates that the candidate is not very keen on bagging the job and is sitting there just for the sake of appearing at the job interview. It also shows that you are ready to walk out any moment the interview is over which is obviously not a healthy sign.

Body Language Pitfalls you must avoid

During the interview consider the following body language red flags. Avoid them because they send out meanings that you don't want to deliver in an interview. Keep in mind that a job interview is a formal communication. You cannot afford to break your chance just because you have a bad habit you could not get rid of.

Pointing

During the interview, the recruiter sets a distance between him and the applicant. This is to keep things professional. Although not obviously, pointing your finger at the person you are talking to breaks that space. The act in itself is accusatory and blaming, so avoid doing this during the interview.

Crossing the arms over the chest

Crossing your arms over your chest is a very defensive gesture. It's as if you do not want the interviewer to know anything about you, which cannot be because the purpose of the interview is to let them know how you can contribute to their company. On top of that, this gesture will make the recruiter feel like you are overriding his authority, as if whatever you say is right and you do not care what he thinks about it.

Fidgeting

Fidgeting is a very distracting body language and it delivers the message that you are not confident. Examples of fidgeting are nail biting, wringing your hands, continuously tapping your feet, and playing with the seams of your suit.

Nodding too much

Nodding too much is a common mistake among applicants. In their desire to let the interviewer know that they are listening and that they understand, they always nod. The problem here is it distracts the interviewer and instead of thinking that you indeed comprehend what he is telling you, he will think of the opposite: you don't really understand that's why you keep on nodding!

Hands behind the back or inside the pockets

Like crossing the arms, hands in the pocket or at your back means that you are unwilling to be approached. Most applicants do this to prevent themselves from fidgeting; but still, this is a major body language red flag. The interviewer will feel like you are holding back and your lack of comfort will dominate the whole interview.

Staring

Because you do not want to break the eye contact, you opt for staring too much! Don't do that, for one thing, that's a creepy gesture and second, it will look like you are the one who is scrutinizing the interviewer. Just be natural and don't forget to blink.

Mismatched facial expression

Sometimes, what your voice implies seem different from what your expression shows. Doing this (even though most of the time it is unintentional) will make the recruiter think that you are pretentious. Don't be too caught up on the rule that you have to smile. If what you are talking about is a serious discussion, opt for a serious expression and soften it if the conversation shifts to a more pleasant track.

Chapter 9: The Worst Things You Can Do

Lack of Preparation

Arriving unprepared is one of the most egregious mistakes you can make. It will be obvious you are having trouble with your answers. The competition is too stiff to not come prepared and knowledgeable about the company you are applying for.

You can do this in a variety of ways but make sure you are prepared for the questions about why you want to work there and what you can offer the company. If you are not prepared, you will also come off as unconfident and that translates badly as well.

Arriving Late or Too Early

The first impression is a lasting one and by being late, you have essentially ended your chance with that company. Arriving late is disrespectful and rude to the person interviewing you. Arriving too early can be a problem as well. If you arrive so early that the interviewer has to rearrange schedules, you are going to be a hindrance to them and not looked at positively.

Arriving on time or a few minutes ahead is the best way to mitigate this problem. You can go so far as to scope out the location beforehand so you know exactly how much time you need to get there, prepare the night before so you are not running late, and have directions in case you get lost.

You also want to be calm when you arrive so being on time means you cannot be flustered and annoyed so make sure that you did prepare the night before so you are relaxed.

Poor Attitude

This is where behavior comes into play. You do not just have to have the right mental mindset, but display it as well. You may not have a poor attitude but your body language suggests you do. You do not want to send the wrong message by slouching, avoiding eye contact, folding your arms, fiddling with your hair or other objects, speaking inaudibly, or using works such as "like" or "um."

Practicing your interview can help with this and making sure you constantly check your posture can help make sure you give the right message with your body.

Unprepared for Questions

You want to sell the idea that you are the perfect candidate for the job. You cannot do that by stumbling all over your words and questions. You need to be prepared for what might be asked of you and know how to form an intelligent, articulate answer to that question.

Prepare and practice is the best method to successful answers. Think through what you might want to know about a candidate and answer those questions. Give solid, positive answers and make sure you make the interviewer see that you are the best candidate.

Inappropriate Attire

Many people know that dressing appropriately is an important part of an interview, but some do not know what "appropriately" means. You need to dress to impress and avoid loud, colorful or tasteless clothing. There is an array of things to avoid like: strong perfume or cologne, nail polish that draws attention, too much jewelry, obvious tattoos, men with piercings visible, etc.

You want the interview to be focused on you, not what you are wearing. Many judgments can be made based on what you are wearing and how you present yourself. If done well, you make a great impression. If done poorly, you will be talked about and not in a good way.

Salary Focus

Money is something you stay away from until the interviewer brings it up. If you are too focused on salary or benefits, you are telling your interviewer that the job means nothing to you and you are after a pay check. You should never ask questions like, "what is my salary?" "How soon will I be promoted?" "How soon can I take vacation?"

These are all things that indicate you are not serious about your career or the job. By having an employee that is self-centered and focused on the perks, the company will not gain anything. You will not be able to sell yourself as a candidate if these types of questions are asked.

Improper Documentation

Just because you have been called does not mean that the person interviewing you received the actual resume. Make sure you have the documents you need to be prepared. Bring extra resumes and reference lists. You cannot be too prepared. Assume that the person you are meeting has nothing to work with.

Perhaps you are meeting with a panel and did not know it. You should have several copies of your resume so you have the ability to show that you are prepared. This will make a huge impression and work well in your favor.

Dishonesty and Rudeness

Attitude has a lot to do with who is hired and who is not. Do not lie. With modern technology, many things can be verified and lying in the interview or on your resume will be found out. Once you have been caught lying, the game is over. You have ruined your chances permanently with that company.

Get caught lying

A definite guarantee that you will not get the job is to lie during the job interview. If you are going to make a bold claim or state something that is not true, seriously think about your chances of getting away with it. Companies run background checks on potential hires. Whether it is about your credentials, accomplishments or your work history, honesty will usually be the best policy.

Inappropriate humor.

Be confident, but avoid cracking jokes unnecessarily or saying things probably best left unsaid. A little touch of humor could work in your favor, provided that it is appropriate to the context of the interview. You do not need to be funny, especially when it is at the expense of appropriateness and formality. The last thing you want is for the hiring manager to think you are not serious about the job opportunity.

Getting personal.

A job interview is a formal meeting to assess if you are the right fit for a job. Everything in your personal life, your subjective opinions and how you are feeling should be left outside the door, and not be brought up during the interview.

Appearing arrogant and entitled.

No one owes you a job; you have to earn the opportunity. If you really are the right candidate for the job, your credentials and professionalism will speak for itself. You appear full of yourself if you make inflated claims about your qualifications, bad mouth previous employers or make assumptions about the job role.

Ask when the interview will end.

Nothing says "I don't care about this job and I am just wasting your time" like asking the interviewer how long the interview will be, or when will it end. You will also be doing just as much damage by constantly looking at your watch. When you are called in for a job interview, you are expected to make time for it, if you really want to get the job.

Chapter 10: How To Relay Your Answers

Try to answer questions using only positive language and avoid negative words such as: problems, conflict, disappointment etc.

Interviewers will often use a technique called "projection questions". You can be asked a question that initially seems not to apply to you directly. Here are a few tips on how to answer the questions:

Address The Interviewer The Same As they Introduce Themselves

Have you ever noticed that most people prefer to be called by their first name? When last did you hear someone instruct you to refer to him or her with his or her last name? The main reason for this is that using the last name when addressing someone is a show of respect. In a world where little of this is going around, you are more likely to stand out from the crowd. NB: throughout your interview, the interviewer will be trying to assess how easy it will be to manage and work with you. As much as employers are looking for leaders and self-starters, sometimes they need someone who can do his/her job and act like a soldier. If the interviewer introduces themselves as Mr Smith, or Ms Johnson, address them as that name during the interview. Don't suddenly call them Andrew or Jessica just because you are aware of their first name.

Look People in The Eye

As a point of emphasis, body language is very important when it comes to displaying appropriate interview etiquette. Studies have shown that about 80 percent of our conversations are non verbal. One good way to build trust and connect with people is to look them in the eyes. This also applies when you find yourself in a group interview. Most people tend to show nervousness when under pressure, lack confidence and don't usually smile. Something as simple as a friendly smile can make the world of difference in showcasing leadership and confidence, even if you are a nervous wreck.

Let the interviewer lead the interview

If your interviewer appears to be somehow laid back or soft spoken, you may feel the urge to get things moving by trying to take back some control. Before you know it, you are rambling. Overcome this temptation and let the hiring manager run the show. If you experience moments of silence, just embrace the silence. If you are adequately prepared for the interview, then you have nothing to worry about. Talking too much is one of the most common mistakes people get wrong during interviews.

Avoid Interrupting

Some people have a bad habit of interrupting someone else when speaking. This very annoying habit shows lack of courtesy. Let the person interviewing you finish making their point and then add to the conversation or respond to their question.

Sit Up and Lean Slightly Forward

Even if you have the excellent qualifications, you stand a very big chance of being rejected just for being too laid back in the interview, I mean literally. This is one of the most common reasons older candidates are often prejudged as lacking in ambition and drive. However, you also need to be on your guard even if you are a younger job seeker to avoid coming out too relaxed or casual.

Chapter 11: The Secret of Interview Etiquette

How to behave during the interview

Don't try too hard to make the interviewer like you. They may interpret this unfavorably, either deciding that you are desperate to find a job, or that you are somewhat disingenuous. Try just to be calm, confident and professional.

Always try to emit a positive attitude and a feeling of wellbeing throughout the interview process, even if your expression is serious and you don't often smile. Even if you are tired, the feeling of inner happiness will make your eyes shine, which will be received positively by any interviewer.

Always remember that during the interview, the person interviewing you will not only be considering what he or she thinks of you, but will also be considering you from the point of view of their clients.

The best emotion that you can convey at all times is calmness. Only in that state are we capable of thinking clearly and quickly. Also, you will make a much better impression if you talk to the interviewer calmly and patiently.

Principles of Interview Etiquette

Your etiquette determines whether or not you get to the next level of the recruitment process. Most job candidates spend much of their time and energy thinking about their skills and qualifications to present to the interviewer and forget about personal conduct. Good manners determine the success of a business relationship since they determine how you establish rapport with other people.

Your manner of behavior toward others is equally important as your résumé and any kind of experience. It is no surprise, therefore, that recruiters are interested in individuals who will fit within their business family.

The following guidelines reflect the principles of interview etiquette that show you how to avoid some mistakes job hunters have made and which derail them from reaching their goal.

How to greet your interviewers?

Interviewers are most often referred to by their first name. Chances of offending someone by referring to them by their first name are minimal since it is the universal standard of meeting someone for the first time. However, calling someone by their last name shows a sense of respect and it directly tells them that you consider them important. Remember that the employer is looking for suggestions that you will be easy to work with, fully understanding the organizational management structure and respecting it.

Table talk

After greeting, the interviewer should remain standing until or unless you are asked to sit. Once you are offered a seat, refrain from feeling comfortable to the point of placing your belongings, such as a handbag, on the table. Be humble enough to place them under your chair or beside your legs. Only a professional binder should be placed on the table near you. Remember to turn down the offer of a drink politely if one is offered. Finally, sit up properly without moving your feet around.

Ensure your cell phone is completely off

An interview is definitely one of the most crucial gatherings in your life and a phone distraction is not worth ruining such a meeting. Interviewers are keen to notice a phone's vibration; thus, it should be totally off. If possible, do not enter the interview room with your phone. At this moment there is nothing more important than your conversation with your potential employer. They will want to know if you can serve their clients without being distracted by your own personal gadget. Therefore, make sure to avoid the distraction at all costs.

Do not talk over the speaker

The most disturbing aspect in an interview is stepping into the interviewer's last two to three words of a statement and talking over without even extending the courtesy to letting them finish their statement.

Take notes during the interview

One of the items that you should bring with you into an interview room is a professional-looking binder. Remember to make it useful during the conversation. Taking notes indicates that you are candidly interested in the job and the company, and it also helps you to pose a query when you are given a chance. Talking of an official folder, invest in one that looks first class. Do not use an electronic gadget such as a tablet to take notes in the interview. Such gadgets can only be used if you are interviewing for an Information Technology position or something similar. Also, remember that providing your professional references and résumé copies is a positive note.

Chase the position tirelessly even if you feel like the interview has already gone wrong

It is not unusual for someone to be having a rough time during an interview and to even create conclusions about the company, which may impact their ability to deliver the best version of themselves. The best thing you can do during such a time is to maintain professionalism and finish the interview without showing any signs of backing down.

Remember that your interview is not over until you walk out of the gate

From the moment you walk through the gate, how you talk to the receptionist or any other person, including the premises' cleaners, matters a lot in your hiring process. Some employers have taken time to ask parties such as the receptionist how you greeted them on your way in. Hiring managers could watch a candidate as they exit the interview premises. Conversely, some interviewees have some outrageous behavior such as starting to make calls or lighting up cigarettes right outside the premises. Remember to maintain official conduct until you are far from the premises.

Close the interview the right way

Express your gratitude toward the interviewer for the interview as it comes to an end and restate your interest in the role. Feel free to make an inquiry on how long it would take before they could reach out. Finally, greet everyone in the room by the hand if possible and also use their name as this shows your attention to details and courtesy. Greeting other people in the outer office shows good manners as well, although it may not be a strategy per se. Remember to keep smiling until you leave the premises.

Chapter 12: Interview Techniques And Tips

Things to Do Before the Job Interview

Research About the Organization and Interviewers

The interview will be smoother if you know the key information about the company. Refer to the organization's website, latest press releases, and social media articles to gain an insight into the company's goals. This can also help you decide if the job is right for you. If any questions pop up during this time, jot them down to look at in the future.

Don't Leave Home without These

Do not face the hiring manager without bringing these job interview essentials. Never forget to bring your CV/resume. Do not assume that just because you e-mailed or sent them a copy already, that your interviewer would obviously have a copy printed out already. Print out more than enough copies for the number of interviewers you have as well as for yourself.

Make sure that the printouts are clear and the papers are not folded or creased when you hand them out. You should also print out as many copies of your cover letter to go with your resumé. Also, have on hand a list of your references including their names, positions and contact details.

Confirm

Keep in mind to call the office of the hiring manager the day before your scheduled interview. This is common courtesy and shows that you are organized and respectful of your appointments. It also allows you to truly confirm your schedule and make any adjustments in advance should any problems arise. It is possible that your interview schedule may have been overlooked by a secretary or the date is incorrect due to a typo error in an e-mail sent to you.

Practice Answering Common Questions

Prepare yourself for answering the most common questions and topics that are discussed in interviews. These include: "Tell us about yourself," "Why you are interested in taking up this position in our company?" and "Why are you the best candidate?" Present a positive image of yourself and talk about how you can contribute to the organization. Remember to focus on what you can do for them, not what they can do for you

Read the Job Description Carefully

You can print out the description of the job and read through it thoroughly. Underline the specific skills the employer is looking for in a candidate. Think about some things from your previous and current jobs that align with the job requirements. Try to come up with concrete examples to use in the interview.

Use the STAR Method for Answering Questions

You will almost certainly be asked to describe a previous experience where you used a specific skill, so you should be prepared to tell stories of your past work experience. Follow the STAR technique where you first describe the situation, then the task, the action you took, and the final result.

Use the Help of a Friend

Practicing is most effective when you say the answers out loud. You can either say them in front of a mirror or ask a friend to help you with the answers. In this way, you will gain confidence and be well prepared for the interview. If you do enlist the help of a friend, show them the job description and help them brainstorm potential questions for you to practice answering.

Prepare a Reference List

You may be asked to give some references prior to or after the interview. If your reference list is ready beforehand, the hiring process may move more quickly. Be sure to contact your references before submitting your list to the employer. Make sure they are willing to be a reference for you.

Keep Examples of Work Ready

You will probably be asked to show some past work you have done that is related to this job. After you have reviewed the job description, think about the work you have done in clubs, volunteer positions, or past jobs that shows you are prepared for and have the experience necessary to be successful at the job.

Be Ready to Ask Smart Questions

Interviews involve a conversation between the interviewers and the interviewee, so you are expected to ask some pertinent questions to show your genuine interest in the organization and position. Be prepared to ask some smart questions to show off your skills and impress your employers.

Tips for the Day of the Interview

Plan Your Attire Beforehand

If possible, find out about the company's dress code for the workplace and dress accordingly. You can try to talk to someone who works there, or you can do some research to find an appropriate outfit. It is better to be overdressed than underdressed. Prepare your outfit the night before so you do not have to worry about clothes on the day of your interview.

Things to Take to the Interview

You should take a minimum of five printed copies of your resume if there are multiple interviewers. You can highlight some specific accomplishments in your personal copy so that you may refer to it and discuss it during the interview.

Take a notebook and pen to jot down points during the interview. These will be useful during the follow-up process.

Be Honest

Do not lie to the interviewer. In this digital age, information is readily and easily accessible to anyone who needs it. Be careful with the data you put on your resume for these can be verified through different sources.

Turn Off Your Cellphone

It is common knowledge that it would indeed be very be rude to take a call, or even read an SMS or e-mail during a job interview. Just turn off that thing! If you cannot afford to do so, then switch it to silent mode. Turn off any alarms you have set on your phone, too. Your phone ringing could possibly disrupt your conversation with the hiring manager and disturb an interview that is actually going pretty well.

Listen: Be polite and mind your manners

Listen first to what your interviewer has to say before you go ahead and speak. Do not talk over him or interrupt him when speaking.

Do Not Talk Too Much

Applicants who rambled on and on about a particular topic might turn off job interviewers. Notice when you are already repeating yourself or talking in a loop or taking a pretty long time to answer a simple question. This usually shows that you do not know the answer to a question and the words coming out of your mouth are empty. Sometimes, it might be due to nervousness caused by the interview itself or perhaps the lie that you are telling. So compose yourself before continuing to answer a question.

Arrive Early

Punctuality is key. At any cost, do not be tardy. It is a sign that you are unreliable and unprofessional.

Plan your schedule so that you arrive at least ten to fifteen minutes early. If you are using public transportation, have a backup plan in case there are sudden closures or delays.

Make a Fantastic First Impression

Be careful about the little things. See to it that your shoes are shining, there are no holes or stains on your clothes, and your nails are not dirty. Dress appropriately and try to look professional. Keep a smile on your face and exhibit confidence by standing tall.

Behave in a Courteous Manner

Treat everyone with respect including the people you meet in the parking lot, at the security station, and at the front desk. The potential employer may ask them for feedback about you.

Display Positive Body Language

Walk and sit in a confident manner and keep your back straight. You can manage your anxiety and nervousness by breathing deeply and exhaling slowly. Shake hands with the interviewer and smile.

Remember the Four C's for Communication.

Clear: Ensure that the statements you make are clear. It should not be possible to interpret them in various ways.

Concise: You should be brief. You need not elaborate on things and give countless details unless it is necessary or you have been asked to do so.

Coherent: See to it that there is a flow to your statements. They should be connected in a coherent manner.

Complete: You should tell the complete story without leaving out the essential bits of information.

Be Authentic and Positive

You can win over the employers by being sincere and genuine during the conversation. Displaying positivity with good body language and a smile can help keep the interview flowing in a constructive and light direction.

Be honest about your accomplishments and skills. Do not exaggerate them, but do not undersell yourself. Focus on the key strengths you have that make you the right fit for the job. Explain the way that the strengths are related to the goal of the company or department and how they may be beneficial for the employer.

Support Your Answers with Examples

Give examples from your previous jobs where you successfully performed tasks related to this job description. Include concrete and quantifiable data to demonstrate your specific accomplishments.

Give Concise and Pertinent Answers

Do not waste time rambling. This is why it is important to practice your answers so that you can respond in an appropriate and relevant manner without taking too much time for each answer. Unless you are asked for a detailed answer, spend only two or three minutes on each answer.

Do Not Say Negative Things About Previous Employers

Organizations like to hire people who are problem solvers and can overcome difficult situations. They do not wish to hire people who cannot get along with others or have a habit of blaming others for their shortcomings. So if you criticize your previous supervisors or employers, you may not be hired. Remain as positive as possible even if your previous employer was unpleasant.

Ask About the Subsequent Steps

You may ask the interviewer, recruiter, or hiring manager what you are expected to do after the interview. You may have to provide a reference list, write some assignment, or appear for another interview.

Avoid swearing

Unless a ceiling panel falls on your head and you need to be rushed to the hospital because of the gash, there is pretty much no excuse for using any expletives during your interview. Even if you're relating a true story, omit the curse words.

Avoid sexist and racist language.

In fact, avoid any language or terms that could potentially offend anyone. You have no idea how people feel about any of those things, whether or not they have friends or spouses of one persuasion or another, or pretty much anything at all. If you offend someone in your interview you can kiss the job goodbye.

Avoid personal details.

Employment law states that you cannot be asked if you're married, how many children you have, if you care for elderly parents or a disabled family member, or pretty much anything having to do with your personal life.

Send a Thank You Note

You can send letters or emails to each of the interviewers to thank them individually. You can use the notes taken in the course of the interview and create distinct emails for each interviewer.

Chapter 13: How To End The Job Interview Properly

Once you have done the interview, it is always a good way to go out with a thank you. Thank the interviewer for his or her time. Also, the end of the interview signifies the end of the formal conversation that you had with the interviewer but not their process of choosing the right candidate.

Take this opportunity to ask a few questions, like when and how you would know the result of the interview and if there are any other things that you can do for them like submit another form of paperwork or anything at all. Just be careful not to overdo it and avoid asking questions like anything that is related to the pay-that is an appropriate question for a different time.

You should also know that there would be more to the selecting process other than the interview proper. You should prove to them that you are worth their time by not appearing anything near unprofessional. Constantly calling them and asking if you got selected or not will not help you much. In fact, it is most likely going to ruin your chances. Instead, you should just wait at least a few weeks if you really want a go signal to go looking for other interviews. But if you did everything right, the chances are you succeeded in that interview and that you get the position you were interviewing for.

When ending the interview, the important thing is to leave your interviewer with the right picture of you. Showing some good etiquette is the way to go. It will leave a lasting impression about you that might just help you clinch the job. Don't forget to shake hands with your interviewer and thank him for the time spent with you.

Be courteous with everyone you meet on your way out. Maybe some of them will be your team mates if you get hired. Don't remove your jacket or take off those heels until you are out of the building.

You have this one last chance to sell yourself to the interviewer and leave him pondering about you long after you've left. By closing the interview properly, you get to score extra points with the interviewer.

Here are some expert tips on how to successfully close an interview:

Never Leave the Interview with Nothing

You need to get the names and position and of everyone you met during the job interview. By everyone, it means all the people you came across with including those whom you thought are insignificant or unimportant. You never know, they may come in handy later. – Usually you will get a business card, if not, make a point of asking for names and write them down.

Don't Forget to Ask for the Next Steps

Don't hesitate to ask what the next steps are in their hiring process: Will they call back the top raking candidates for another interview? How soon will the company make a hiring decision? When can we expect the hiring manager to move to this next step?

These are the questions you should ask at the end of the interview. Don't worry, it is totally appropriate for you to ask such questions.

Confirm Your Interest in the Job

Closing an interview gives you an opportunity to let the interviewer know how enthusiastic you are with the job. Take this moment to let him know how the interview got you more interested in the job.

Don't Forget to Ask for the Job

Whatever closing style you use or however you want to close the interview, you must remember some important key points:

- Make sure the interviewer profiled you the way you want him to. There should be at least five of your skill sets or personality traits you want him to remember you with after the interview.
- Volunteer to provide him with additional references, background information or even work samples.
- Express your deep interest for the job without sounding like an eager beaver. Remind him of the added value you can contribute to the company.
- Don't forget to ask what the next step in the hiring process is. Try to secure the decision date so you'd know when to follow it up.
- Get their complete contact details so you'll know how and who to contact if you don't hear from them in time.

Ask if they need any final information

At the end of the interview this is a great question to ask, it may seem really simple but it's super powerful. You will gauge how well you have done by asking this question. At the end of your interview, always ask:

"Do you need any additional information from my side".

When you ask this question you can watch the body language of the interviewers. You will be able to ascertain how well you performed, the reason being. By asking this question you are physiologically asking the interviewers if they liked you or not.

Closing an interview gives you an opportunity to let the interviewer know how enthusiastic you are with the job. Take this moment to let him know how the interview got you more interested in the job.

There are many ways and styles to close the interview as you've seen above. However, the closing style you choose to use must be custom-fitted to the position you are applying for, to your unique personality, and to the interviewing style and personality of the interviewer. Choose the most appropriate closing style to use that fits the situation to a tee.

You need not stop talking to the interviewer even after the interview has ended. Continue the conversation by engaging him in small talk. Show him that you want to be friends even after the interview. This will leave a lasting impression something he can remember you with.

Chapter 14: After The Interview

Even though the interview is over, the process is not quite finished. Here are a few suggestions on what comes next.

Follow up immediately with a thank you note and summarize the interview. This step will put your name and visit back in the mind of the interviewer. It shows that you appreciate their time and the opportunity to interview for the position. In a close tie between applicants, this could be the small detail that tips the decision in your favor.

Update your question list with any new questions that you think could have helped you gain more information. It is also a good time to update your personal folder with any information that the interviewer requested that you did not have included. All of your documents will change as time passes and it is important to keep them updated.

Keep looking for other opportunities. You do not want to wait around in case they never get back to you. Even if they respond and you accept the offer, it is not a big deal to cancel any other interviews that you also have scheduled.

Making Follow Ups

By making follow-ups, you will be refreshing the interviewer's mind that you are one of the best choices to hire. You will also be strengthening your position as the best candidate who is a perfect fit for the job and that they should consider your application seriously. Your thank you note only goes to show that you're extremely interested in the position.

Here are some pointers on how to make the follow ups:

- A thank you email sent immediately after the interview is the way to go. It is the quickest and the most convenient way of saying thank you. Thank you email messages are appropriate too in all cases.
- A handwritten thank you message sent to the interviewer or the hiring manager will add a personal touch to your message. Writing a personalized thank you message, putting it in an envelope and stamping it, then mailing it will prove to the company that you so highly regard the job that you are willing to spend time sending them a thank you note like that. It will also serve as an additional reminder that you are a serious contender for the job.
- Making a follow-up phone call can boost your chances of landing the job especially if the job entails of phone time. Making follow-up phone calls gives you the opportunity to showcase your strong communication skills which may be required for the position. You can highlight once more a few of your key qualifications in addition to saying thank you for seriously considering you for the job. You can also mention other important things which you forgot to say during the interview.

After Landing the Job

Even after the interviewing process is complete, make sure to keep your personal folder updated regularly. It is much easier to incrementally update it than update it all at once when you start your next job search.

This tactic also makes it easier for you to remember everything that should be included. You do not want to miss out on a future opportunity because you forgot to include a project that would have shown valuable experience for your next position.

Final Conclusion

Firstly, thank you for making it through to the end of this book. I hope this book has helped you know what you can do and what to avoid in order to ace that interview. Now you can be sure that with the tips you have learnt here, you will never fail to pass an interview again.

You should now have a good understanding of how job interviews are conducted and how to prepare for them. After reading this book, you should be able to ace your next interview and land your dream job with great ease.

I felt it best to cover all aspects of the interview process, from the very basics to the intricate details required. What I find is that all walks of life need a refresher when it comes to interviews. We all need a little reminder of what we need to do in order to get the job. In retrospect it's usually the more experienced folks who need a reminder more than the young guns.

I smile writing this section as you may have noticed I said more experienced rather than older! Anyway, I think sometimes we all get set in our ways, interviews have pretty much the same theme and certainly not rocket science. It's all about selling yourself to the folks around the table, leave nothing out and prepare properly.

At the end of the day, if you prepare correctly which isn't hard, and you go in with a smile and some confidence, you have done all you can to get the job. The point is, leave nothing off the table, it will put you in good stead with or without the job. Don't presume anything!, tell your story.

The main failure of folks who fail interviews are, they expect the interviewer to understand what is going on within their brains.

They expect interviewers to know how good they are. Well, sorry to be blunt that just does not happen. You have to remember, generally, the interviewer has no idea who you are, or how good you are. If you don't sell yourself, someone else will!. Make it your job, tell yourself, this is my job!.

You are great at what you do, you should be proud of who you are, you are a great person! Go and show what you can do and get your dream job!

Printed in Great Britain
by Amazon